Wedding Speeches

A Practical Guide for Delivering an Unforgettable Wedding Speech

Tips and Examples for
**Father of the Bride Speeches,
Mother of the Bride Speeches,
Father of the Groom Speeches,
Mother of the Groom Speeches,
Groom Speeches, Bride Speeches,
Best Man Speeches and
Maid of Honor Speeches**

By Sam Siv

Your wedding day should be the most important day of your life. It is the day when all your friends and family, as well as the friends and family of your husband-to-be, gather together to celebrate your big day. Unless you are lucky enough to be able to afford a wedding planner, you will have so many things to think about and plan, from the pre-wedding parties to the wedding ceremony and reception, and even the honeymoon.

As part of your wedding day, it is expected that certain people in your wedding party give speeches to congratulate you on your newly married status and also to tell a few stories about you and the groom. To a certain extent, you don't need to worry about this aspect of the wedding, unless you intend to make a speech yourself. However, you will want to have an input into who makes the speeches and how long they are because this will have a roll-on effect on everything else that happens at your wedding reception.

Who gives the speeches and toasts at your wedding really depends on what you want. It is traditional for the male side of the wedding party only to give speeches. You may even want to cut this down further and just ask the best man and groom to give a speech. Then again, you may want to laugh in the face of tradition and make sure the female side of the wedding party, including yourself, have the chance to say something. Of course, you will need to check with everyone that they are happy to give a speech. The groom and best man probably won't have much choice, but others may prefer to stay quiet and simply listen to what the main members of the wedding party have to say.

See Sam Siv's other Wedding Books on Amazon.com

Sign up to receive motivational quotes and special offers from Sam Siv.

Table of Contents

Introduction for the Bride and Groom

Your wedding day should be the most important day of your life. It is the day when all your friends and family, as well as the friends and family of your husband-to-be, gather together to celebrate your big day. Unless you are lucky enough to be able to afford a wedding planner, you will have so many things to think about and plan, from the pre-wedding parties to the wedding ceremony and reception, and even the honeymoon.

As part of your wedding day, it is expected that certain people in your wedding party give speeches to congratulate you on your newly married status and also to tell a few stories about you and the groom. To a certain extent, you don't need to worry about this aspect of the wedding, unless you intend to make a speech yourself. However, you will want to have an input into who makes the speeches and how long they are because this will have a roll-on effect on everything else that happens at your wedding reception.

Who gives the speeches and toasts at your wedding really depends on what you want. It is traditional for the male side of the wedding party only to give speeches. You may even want to cut this down further and just ask the best man and groom to give a speech. Then again, you may want to laugh in the face of tradition and make sure the female side of the wedding party, including yourself, have the chance to say something. Of course, you will need to check with everyone that they are happy to give a speech. The groom and best man probably won't have much choice, but others may prefer to stay quiet and simply listen to what the main members of the wedding party have to say.

You may also want to have an idea of what people are planning to say. This all depends on your personality and that of the groom. If you are shy and retiring, for example, you may want the speech givers to tone down what they are going to say and not cite any embarrassing incidents from the past. If you believe that they may say something you really don't want them to say, you will need to be honest with them right from the start.

On the other hand, you may have a great sense of humor and be more than happy for people to recount embarrassing stories from your past; you may even want to remind them of these stories to ensure then are included. Few speech givers will speak off-the-cuff, so making it clear in advance should give them plenty of time to prepare their speeches.

Remember that your wedding reception is almost certainly going to be filmed and you will have both the memory and the evidence of the speeches that people make for the rest of your life. Even if you don't hire a videographer, someone will undoubtedly film the speeches and may even put them on YouTube. Do yourself a favor by giving the speech givers a handle on what you do and don't want them to say so that your wedding speeches are something you are not embarrassed to look back on in due course.

Some people are natural public speakers; others aren't. The first stage is obviously to research write the speech, which can tie some people up in knots. The second stage is to practice, practice, and practice – possibly in front of other people so that they can give plenty of feedback. The final stage is actually delivering the speech, which can be the hardest part for someone who is not a natural public speaker.

This e-book will give tips on how to choose people to give wedding speeches and toasts and the etiquette involved if you decide that you want to follow tradition. It will also provide tips for each member of the wedding party on researching and writing their speeches. This will include the father and mother of the bride, father and mother of the groom, the bride and groom themselves, the bridesmaids/maid of honor, and finally the best man.

Each member of the wedding party has been designated their own chapters full of tips and examples of what to say. Of course, this will need to be amended to suit each person's personality, but it will at least provide a starting point, if only to give each person a definite idea of what they don't want to say. Examples of speeches include both straight and funny versions so that each person can decide whether they would best suit one or the other. Finally, each chapter will be written from the point of view of the person who will be giving the speech, so you, as the bride, can hand out the relevant chapters to the relevant people.

We hope that this e-book provides plenty of ideas for you and your loved ones when it comes to giving speeches at your wedding.

Chapter 1. Order of the Speeches

The order of the speeches at your wedding reception really depends on whether the wedding is traditional, or whether the bride is happy to have a more informal one. This is entirely up to the bride and her husband-to-be, although it may be advisable for them to ask their parents for their views, especially if they are contributing towards the cost of the wedding. The bride and groom will also want to consider the theme of the wedding; for example, it may make more sense to have no more than a couple of speeches at a beach wedding when everyone is dressed in shorts and a tee-shirt.

Traditional Wedding

At a traditional wedding, the order of the speeches would usually be the father of the bride, followed by the father of the groom, the groom himself and then the best man. The first three speeches will usually be relatively short, with the best man's speech saved as the piece de resistance at the end. Unless there is a master of ceremonies, such as the band leader or DJ, the father of the bride would introduce each speech in turn.

However, this really does depend on who has contributed the most to the cost of the wedding. Traditionally, that would be the father of the bride, but in this day and age, many brides and grooms pay for their own weddings. In that case, it will make more sense for the groom to give the first speech and introduce the others. In the case that the father of the groom has contributed the most to the cost of the wedding, it should obviously be the father of the groom who acts as the host. These are all points to discuss in advance, however, because some fathers of the bride may not want it to be known that they have not contributed financially towards the wedding.

Informal Wedding

At a more informal wedding, anything really goes. It may make most sense for the bride and the groom themselves to act as hosts and introduce the different speeches. However, it may not be necessary to have hosts at all if the bride and groom don't want anything too starchy; they may prefer people who have something to say about you to just stand up and say it. They should just bear in mind that this will only really work if the wedding is an intimate one in an informal location. If people need to be out of the venue by a certain time, it is much more advisable to have a plan to adhere to.

Female Members of the Wedding Party

It is not traditional for female members of the wedding party to give any kind of speech at a wedding reception. Public speaking would usually be left to the male side of the wedding party. However, women's independence has come a long way over the past few decades and it is now becoming more acceptable for the mothers of the bride and groom, the bride herself, and even the bridesmaids to give speeches.

If it is decided that the female side of the wedding party to give speeches, the usual order of all the speeches would be as follows:

- Father of the bride
- Mother of the bride
- Father of the groom
- Mother of the groom
- Groom
- Bride

- Best Man
- Bridesmaids/Maid of Honor

That is, of course, a lot of speeches to get through; even if each person only speaks for three or four minutes, there could easily be over half an hour of speeches, by which time the guests could be bored out of their minds. Bear in mind that it is incredibly hard to keep a speech to just a few minutes and some people will go well over. It will then be hard to ask them to stop mid-speech and then there's hardly any time left for other activities.

It may then make more sense for either the father or mother of the bride and either the father or mother of the groom to give speeches, followed by the bride and then the best man. The bride and groom should play around with ideas, depending upon who will give the best speeches, and come up with a plan to suit their personal situation.

Variations

It may be tradition to have one speech after another, usually before the dinner commences, but there is nothing to say that things can't be changed around. If, for example, the bride and groom want several speeches, but aren't sure that the guests will enjoy sitting still for long periods of time; the speeches could be staggered so that each speech takes place before a particular part of the wedding reception.

As an illustration, the father and mother of the bride could give a speech when guests have arrived at the wedding reception while having cocktails, the groom's father and/or mother could give a speech when all the guests are seated, then the bride and groom could make a speech after the main course, with the best man's speech at the end of the meal before the dancing begins.

Another option is to not have speeches as such at all, but to organize a presentation of the bride and groom's lives. Different members of the wedding party could step in and say a few words as photographs of different stages of their lives are shown. This may even involve people outside of the immediate wedding party, such as grandparents, aunts and uncles, siblings, friends and even work colleagues.

Having 'mini-speeches' illustrated by photographs can be a lot more fun than boring speeches and has a much less formal feel. There is also the added advantage that the bride and groom can ask to vet the slides of the presentation in advance!

Choosing the right people to give speeches at a wedding is far more important than following order and protocol. What the bride and groom decide works best at their wedding is really up to them. They will just need to manage expectations, so that if they decide they don't want your groom's father to give a speech, he knows in plenty of time. If they think they are going to cause offence by not including people, it may be better to just let them speak, but insist that they stick to a very tight time slot.

Chapter 2. How to Deliver a Great Speech

Whatever your role at the wedding, if you have been asked to give a speech, you will need to think through what you are going to say very carefully. You may think that you are already a good public speaker, but when it comes to giving a speech at a wedding, you may find that you need to completely rewrite your rule book. For a start, you are probably used to giving speeches to a particular group of people; for example, your work colleagues, or students you will have a good idea of what will appeal to them and what won't. When it comes to wedding guests, it could be a whole different ballgame. There are a number of things that you should do in order to deliver a great speech.

Research

It doesn't matter how good you are at giving off-the-cuff speeches, if you have been honored with being asked to speak at someone's wedding, you need to make sure that say the right things and you can only do that if you have done your research. Firstly, make sure you know exactly who is going to be there. If you know everyone really well, then it may be permissible to be cheeky in your speech, but if you know the groom's mother is going to take great offence if you say anything negative about her son, even in a tongue-in-cheek way, then you should tone your speech down immediately.

Of course, the main people you want to please are the bride and groom and whoever is contributing the most towards the cost of the wedding. This could be particularly important; you don't, for example, want to make a joke about the cheap floral arrangements if the bride's mother and grandmother spent hours arranging the flowers themselves. Think before you speak and, if you aren't sure, then it may be better to leave what you were going to say out completely.

The same goes for telling stories about the bride. You may find the stories hilarious, and so might your close friends, possibly even the bride herself, but it doesn't mean everyone will find them so. Remember that you are taking part in an important event, one that will almost certain be filmed and remembered in years to come, so you want to do your best to make it a memorable one. Don't take any chances; you can leave the dirty stories to your yearly barbecue if you really must rake them up.

Another thing to find out is how long the bride wants you to speak for. It is then important to stick to her guidelines. There is probably a timeframe by which you all need to have left the building and if you keep talking for too long, there may not be time for other people's speeches.

Finally, make sure you know exactly how many people to whom you will be talking and whereabouts the key players will be sitting. You will almost certainly be on the same table as the rest of the main wedding party, but there may be other people you wish to direct your speech towards; for example, grandparents and close family friends. This can make a difference when it comes to delivering your speech, because it will help if you can look at them as you are speaking about them. The number of guests is also important so that you can practice how much to raise your voice. You will also want to find out if there will be microphones available.

Preparation

Once you know all you can about your audience, you can start preparing your speech. When it comes to finding clever and witty things to say, there are plenty of websites online that will give you examples and, if you look at the relevant chapter in this e-book, you will find examples of introductions to each section of your speech that you could make. However, you will want to make the speech your own, so don't be tempted to take any examples you find without customizing them. Think about what you know about the bride and groom and only use examples that you find as a template for a personal speech that you give from the heart.

The key to writing a speech is to leave plenty of time before the wedding to start drafting it. That is particularly important if you are nervous. You may need several sittings before you are finally ready to start practicing and, even then, you will probably need to keep revisiting it. Whether you initially decide to write your speech out in full, or just have a few bullet points, is really up to you and your comfort levels. If you're relatively new to public speaking, you may find that writing it out in full helps you to concentrate and practice different nuances, but if you're well-practiced, you may prefer to just have a few keywords on which to base what you say.

Practice

Once your speech is largely ready, it is time to start practicing it. To begin with, unless you are really confident, just practice on your own. It will give you time to get used to hearing your own voice and to think about whether what you have prepared sounds right out loud. Then practice in front of a friend or two to see what they think. They will then be able to tell you if anything that you have prepared is out of order and likely to offend the bridal couple.

There will usually be a wedding rehearsal a day or so before the wedding and you may want to practice your speech there. It really depends on whether the bride and groom want to hear what you have to say or not; they may prefer to wait until the day itself. If you do get to practice your speech there, it's worth keeping a few things back because good speeches should evoke emotion and, if the main bridal party has already heard the whole thing, they may just look bored on the day. That won't look good to the other guests and it may put you off your stride.

Delivering on the Day

If you have had plenty of time to practice your speech, your delivery on the day should be polished and confident. However, you are bound to be nervous when faced with so many people, particularly if you know that the bride and groom are relying on you to give a good speech and that you are being filmed. Don't rely on your memory to remember everything that you had to say - nerves may make you forget things. However, don't bring the entire speech written out on several sheets of paper and then bury your head in them while you speak. Instead, just have a couple of prompt cards with bullet points on and refer to them if necessary. Remember to stand up straight and make eye contact with the bridal party and the audience in general.

Giving a speech isn't rocket science, but it may well be more nerve-wracking than you imagined. However, with the help of the Internet, this e-book and plenty of practice in front of other people, there is no reason why your speech shouldn't be a resounding success.

Chapter 3: Tips for Father of the Bride Speeches

If you are the father of the bride, you will almost certainly be expected to give a speech at your daughter's wedding. If you have contributed towards the cost of the wedding, or have been asked to act as host or master of ceremonies, you will probably be the person who opens the speeches and thereafter introduces everyone. You will therefore want to ensure that your speech is well delivered, attracts everyone's attention and hopefully adds a touch of humor to the proceedings too.

As discussed in the previous chapter, you may think that you are a great public speaker; at your stage in life, you probably have a lot of experience of giving presentations in front of a wide range of people. However, you still need to ensure that you prepare in plenty of time if you want to make your daughter happy - and, after all, it should be her only wedding day.

To ensure that your speech is a success, there are a number of things to do and consider.

Who is going to be present?

First of all, check that you know exactly who is going to be present. As the father of the bride, you really ought to know, but if other people have organized the guest list, there may be people you think are coming who aren't. It will be hard to target your speech towards certain people if they are not present. For example, an anecdote about your daughter that involves her cousin may not be appropriate if the cousin is not there, and there may be another story that you could tell that would be more appropriate. There is also little point in thanking someone personally for their contribution to the wedding if they are not there. You can thank them personally at another stage.

Check with your daughter who you should be thanking. She may want you to thank key members of the wedding party for their support in the run-up to the wedding; she may also want you to thank particular vendors who have done a stellar job. Make sure you know everyone's names and have them written down on prompt cards just in case nerves set in.

Welcome and introductions

If you are the first speaker, you will need to presume that not everyone will know who you are. Even if it is a relatively small wedding, there will probably be spouses of guests who don't know you or, indeed, anyone other than their spouse. Make sure that you introduce yourself properly, your role in the proceedings and how the rest of the speeches will work. Then give everyone a warm welcome. There may be a few key people whom you want to thank, but make sure that you thank everyone for attending. At the very least, they took the time to attend your daughter's event and they may well have spent a substantial amount of money on clothes and transportation.

Personal anecdotes about your daughter

You are the best person to talk about your daughter because you know her better than almost everyone. You will almost certainly want to share some details of your daughter's childhood and possible some more recent anecdotes. Remember though that you want to make your daughter smile; you don't want to have her writhing in embarrassment, or to offend her to the extent that she doesn't want to speak to you after the wedding. You may want to discuss the anecdotes you have chosen with her before the big day so that she can ask you to rethink if necessary. If you do decide to go ahead and surprise her, make sure the anecdotes you choose are light-hearted.

What you know about the groom

You will also probably want to say a few words about the groom. This may be easy if you know him well and already consider him to be part of your family. However, if your daughter lives elsewhere, you may only have met the groom a few times. If you don't know the groom all that well, just say a few words about him - perhaps something along the lines of that you haven't known him for long, but you know how much your daughter loves him and that you trust her taste in everything.

When planning your speech, by all means have a little bit of fun at his expense, particularly if you know him well, but don't say anything that is going to cause too much embarrassment. Remember that his friends and family are present and may not appreciate hearing about how he humiliated himself the first time he met you.

Keep it short!

You are the father of the bride and your speech should be one of the highlights, but that doesn't give you the right to talk for so long that everyone becomes bored. Remember that there could be quite a few speeches following yours and it isn't fair to steal their thunder. Ask your daughter how long she wants you to talk and make sure you stick to it. That is where practice comes in; you should soon have a good idea of how much you can say in five minutes.

Toast the bride and groom at the end

You will want to raise a glass to the bride and groom at the end of your speech, as well as the rest of the guests at the wedding. Just like the speech, keep this short. There may be quite a few more toasts to come after yours and you don't want to get everyone too drunk before the best man's speech right at the end.

You will be proud of your daughter and her achievements and will want to ensure that she has a great day. Do this by ensuring that you give an excellent speech that has everyone smiling, laughing and quite possibly shedding a few quiet tears. Your daughter will remember the love in your eyes and your voice for ever more.

Chapter 4. Examples of Father of the Bride Speeches

So you are all ready to start researching your father of the bride speech, but you don't know where to begin. This chapter will provide you with some ideas of things to say, still allowing you to stamp your own personal mark on the speech. Your audience will be able to tell if you lift it word for word from elsewhere because it won't seem to flow properly and will sound insincere. At the same time, there is nothing wrong with looking for inspiration from elsewhere.

Opening Lines

"Ladies and gentlemen, for those of you who don't know me, I am X. As the bride's father, I have the pleasure of giving the first speech. I would like to start by welcoming you all here today. Some of you have come a long way - I know two guests have come from Australia - but whether you've traveled day and night, or have just walked down the road, I would like to thank you all for coming."

"If I could have everyone's attention please...I know everyone hates father of the bride speeches and that you're looking forward to the food and drink, but I promise you all that I'll keep this as short as possible..."

"Ladies and gentlemen, as father of the bride, I'd like to thank you all for coming from near and far to attend my beloved daughter's marriage to X. My wife X and I are delighted to see so many people here - it is a pleasure to see how many people want to celebrate X and X's wedding today. Of course, I'd particularly like to welcome the groom's parents, X and X, and hope that they won't regret becoming linked to us by marriage by the end of today!"

Stories about your daughter

"I cannot tell you how proud I am of my daughter today. Doesn't she look beautiful? It's a far cry from the way she looked at the age of 8 when she was a bridesmaid and fell headfirst into a muddy puddle before the bride managed to walk down the aisle...I've got the photos to prove it just in case anyone wants to see them."

"I will never forget the day that X was born. She wasn't due for another month, so I was shocked to get a phone call at work one day to say that my wife had gone into labor. I rushed to the hospital just a few minutes away by car and was even more shocked to find that our two-person family had already become three. X was ahead of the rest of us that day and she has remained ahead of us all ever since."

"I can remember when X came home after her first date with the groom. I could tell immediately that she was smitten because she didn't stop talking about him. Four days later when he still hadn't called her, she was practically crying herself to sleep. Fortunately, he did call and so continued the relationship that we see before us today."

Introducing the Groom

"Steve has been a permanent fixture in our lives for the past five years, but some of you here may not have met him properly yet. You'll hopefully have time to get to know him a bit better later on today. In the meantime, you should be warned that he's not a fan of baseball, but apart from that, he's a great guy and I'm delighted that he is marrying my daughter."

"As most of you know, X lives in Alaska and doesn't get the chance to come home very often. As a result, we haven't had the chance to get to know the groom as much as we would like. However, every father wants to know that their daughter is going to be looked after and it is obvious that X is kind, considerate and, most importantly, can keep my daughter in the lifestyle to which she has become accustomed!"

Impart some worldly advice

"I've now been married for 25 years and think I'm very good at it. My wife may disagree! But if I was asked to give some advice to the newlyweds in front of me, it would be to avoid going to bed on an argument. X (groom's name), whatever you do, just agree with her before you go to bed! It will save a lot of grief and sleepless nights in the long run!"

"I believe it's part of my duty to give the happy couple some advice on how to have a long and happy marriage. It's simple. Live a lot, love a lot, listen a lot and laugh a lot. Marriage has its ups and downs, but by following those basic rules you should ensure that the ups and more frequent than the downs."

"Traditionally, I'm supposed to impart some advice on how to have a successful marriage. As some of you will know, no one's going to take any notice of me because X's mother and I divorced twenty years ago and I've never remarried. But if she was here today, I'm sure she'd agree that you need to talk everything through. Don't sweep things under the carpet. That's when wounds begin to fester. Be open with each other and I'm sure you'll be married for the rest of your lives."

The Toast

"Ladies and gentlemen, let's make a toast to the bride and groom...to X and X!"

"Come on everyone, please stand up and raise a glass to the happy couple, Mr. and Mrs. X!"

"It's time to propose a toast to X and X! Wishing you many happy years of marriage to come."

Hopefully some of these examples will have inspired you to start writing your own speech. Before you know it, you'll be wowing the wedding guests with your funny, heart-warming speech!

Chapter 5: Tips for Mother of the Bride Speeches

It may not be tradition for the mother of the bride to give a speech and it probably won't be expected, but, as the mother of the bride, you are perfectly at liberty to give one if you want to. After all, you were the one who gave birth to your daughter and the one who wiped away her tears when her first relationship crashed and burned. You may feel that you are even be more entitled to give a speech than the father of the bride if your relationship with your daughter is stronger than that she has with her father. Of course, if the bride's father has passed on, is not present, or is happy to hand over the reins to you, you may be giving the equivalent of the father of the bride speech anyway.

In any case, it has now become more and more common for the mother of the bride to speak at a wedding, along with the mother of the groom, the maid of honor and/or bridesmaids and, of course, the bride herself. Make this clear if anyone tries to tell you otherwise! Etiquette and tradition at weddings are no longer as important as they once were. The key thing to check is that your daughter is happy for you to say a few words. She may want to stick to being as traditional as possible, in which case, you may need to back down. It is your daughter's day, not yours, no matter how important you are to her.

Like everyone else, you should practice your speech in advance to ensure that it sounds right and so that your delivery on the day is as polished as possible. You will want to consider the following:

Ask your daughter's advice

It is advisable to draft your speech in advance and, if you think it necessary, to run it by your daughter before you decide on a final draft. You may want to pick a few anecdotes from her past to recount to the wedding guests and you want to ensure that they are not going to offend or embarrass her on her big day.

Then again, you may want to tug at the heartstrings with your speech, in which case, check that she is happy with this - if she is aiming to have a fun, light-hearted day, she may not want everyone in tears. You don't necessarily need to share the entire speech with her, just give her an idea of the highlights.

Compare and Contrast

It is a good idea to compare speeches with the father of the bride. This could be particularly important if you are divorced. Although your memories of your daughter are likely to be very different, you don't want to find yourself repeating an anecdote that has already been shared. You may also want to thank people, but if the father of the bride has already done so, you will want to keep this very short. You should, however, thank anyone important that the father of the bride has forgotten. It is probably also wise to compare your speech with other speech givers; you really don't want to steal anyone's thunder by covering something that they are already planning to say.

Don't be tempted to disrespect anyone

Your daughter's wedding isn't the time to be disrespectful to anyone. You may have had an acrimonious divorce from the father of the bride, or you may have fallen out with another member of the family through no fault of your own. However, your wedding speech is not the time to bring it up. If you can't say anything nice, don't say anything at all.

Welcome the Groom and his Family

The father of the bride may already have spoken about the groom and welcomed the in-laws, but there's no reason you can't do the same; in fact, it would probably be remiss if you didn't. You should aim, however, to give a slightly different angle. For example, if the father of the bride gave a jocular, teasing version of how the groom came to meet the bride, you could speak about the first time you realized how important your daughter was to him.

Bring in something about the in-laws and how they are now members of the family; you could, for example, talk about something you've learned from them. This could be a particularly nice touch if they are from another culture and are a little bemused by the way that the bride and groom's wedding ceremony is being conducted. If you don't know them very well, make sure that you get their names right!

Don't be too gushing

You are probably hugely proud of your daughter and want everyone to know. That is fine, but don't go too overboard. There is no need to list every single achievement she has made since she came out of the womb. Everyone will know that you are proud of her, but if you go on for too long, they will begin to get restless. Just highlight a couple of her achievements of which you are most proud; for example, her high grades at university, or, if she already has them, her children. Bear in mind that you only have so many minutes in which to speak and you really don't want to go over what you have been allocated.

You also don't want to be so gushing that you end up in tears. It's fine to have a break in your voice occasionally, to make other people cry, or to have a few tears after you've finished, but you don't want to hold up the proceedings because you can't get your act together. It's worth making sure you wear waterproof mascara so that if you do cry, you don't have mascara streaks all down your face!

Consider avoiding a Toast

If you know that there are several more speeches after yours, and the father of the bride has already given one, you might want to avoid giving another toast. If everyone gives toasts, people are going to get bored of them. Instead, just thank everyone for coming and, unless there is a master of ceremonies, introduce the next speaker.

You won't have as many example speeches to consider if you are giving a speech as the mother of the bride, simply because mother of the bride speeches are still relatively rare. Nevertheless, there are enough ideas out there, including those in the following chapter, which should enable you to put together a great speech with your own personal slant on it.

Chapter 6. Examples of Mother of the Bride Speeches

When you draft your wedding speech, you'll probably be concerned about repeating anything already said. You'll probably also want to make sure that your speech is just as memorable, if not more so, than the father of the bride's.

The best way to start is by jotting down a few ideas of stories you can tell and then checking with your daughter and other speech givers that they are appropriate and not repeated elsewhere. Once you have the main sections that you want to share with the wedding guests, you can then fill in the other parts of the speech with the correct platitudes and thanks to other wedding guests.

We suggest that you consider breaking up your speech into the following sections.

Opening Lines

"As X has already explained, I'm X, X's mother. I know it isn't tradition for the bride's mother to give a speech at weddings, but I've never been one to follow etiquette and, sometimes, it's good to forge new family traditions. I hope my daughter and future grandchildren will do the same."

"Good evening everyone and thank you so much for being with us today. Some of you have traveled for miles and I can't tell you how grateful I am. X and X have even traveled all the way from Europe to be with us today."

"Thank you all for sharing this wonderful day with us. Don't worry; I'm going to keep this short because I know you all want to get on with the celebrations!"

Your Daughter's Main Achievements

"I cannot tell you how proud I am of my daughter. She hasn't always had it easy, but she has overcome all obstacles in her path with grace and a good sense of humor. Determined to go back to school as a mature student, she worked her way through college and still managed to graduate at the top of her class."

"It is hard to believe that just 25 years ago, this beautiful woman in front of me was a tiny baby. I've watched her grow and mature with great pride and I am so happy that she has turned into the sensible, caring, confident woman that she is today. I really don't know where she got it from; certainly not her father or I!"

"(Speaking directly to the bride) X, I cannot tell you how moved I was to see you take your vows earlier today. It reminds me of when I gave my own. The difference is that I had no idea what I was doing and nor did your father! It is a miracle that we made it through those early years. You, on the other hand, are so loving and capable that I just know you won't make the mistakes that we did. X (groom's name), I hope you realize just how lucky you are!"

Welcoming the Groom and In-Laws

"I'd like to reiterate my husband's words by welcoming the groom and X and X to our family. It was obvious from the first time we met X (the groom) that he was a perfect fit for our daughter. It's not just that he's kind and caring, but, as everyone knows, X (the bride) can't cook, but X (the groom) is more than prepared to cook for her!"

"It's a real pleasure to introduce the groom's mother and father to you. They have come a long way to attend the wedding today, but we really hope that they will visit more often. X and I share a love of dress-making and have been trading ideas via Skype for some time now. It's great to finally have the chance to meet her in person."

"It's not common these days for a boyfriend to ask his girlfriend's parents for her hand in marriage, but that's exactly what X did. We thought at first that he was going to ask us for money! He was so embarrassed! But he finally got it out and we immediately set his mind at rest."

Closing lines

"I'm not going to take up any more of your time. Suffice it to say that I wish the very best for the married couple and thank you all for coming.

(If you choose to give a toast) "I would like to propose a toast to X and X. God bless you."

"I'm so pleased to see so many friends and relations here today to share in our celebrations. I hope you all enjoy the rest of the evening.

Think carefully about what you want to get across to the wedding guests and plan how you are going to deliver your speech. Then there is no reason why you shouldn't come out with a speech worthy of a standing ovation.

Chapter 7. Tips for Father of the Groom Speeches

As father of the groom, you will probably follow the father of the bride and possibly the mother of the bride too. If, however, you are footing most of the bill and are giving the introductory speech, you may want to refer to the chapters on father of the bride speeches, which will give you a better idea of how to open the proceedings.

If you are the second or third speaker, you will probably be wondering what you can say that is going to be any different from what others have already said. For that reason, it is probably best if you keep your speech relatively short. That doesn't mean that your speech isn't important; simply that you can leave the long introductions to the speakers before you. The other wedding guests will appreciate your thoughtfulness if you do so.

You may also want to compare notes with the father and mother of the bride just to make sure that you cover anything that they don't. You may, for example, want to make more of a deal of the best man, who is probably more familiar to you that he will be to the father of the bride, and may be feeling very nervous knowing that his speech is coming up. There may also be a few people whom you need to thank, particularly if you've arranged a specific part of the wedding that the father of the bride wouldn't know about.

When preparing your speech, you should take the following into consideration.

Introductions

You will probably know an awful lot of the wedding guests. You may even know the vast majority. However, unless it is a very intimate wedding, there will be a few people who have no idea who you are or what your relationship is to the groom. For that reason, you will want to take the time to introduce yourself and explain that you are the father of the groom.

You'll also want to introduce your wife, even if she is going to follow on from you and say a few words herself. Then say a few words about how happy you and your wife are for the married couple and that you are sure they will have a very happy life together.

Personal anecdotes about your son

You won't want to tell a long-winded story about your son and all his milestones as he grew up because you simply won't have time. However, it is worth picking a story or two from his childhood. You could say, for example, that you knew he had an eye for the ladies from an early age, but that as soon as he met his wife, you could tell that she was the one.

You may also want to bring up a couple of his key achievements and say how proud you are of him. Don't start listing all his achievements since he learned to walk, however, because it will just bore everyone. Most of them will probably already know his key achievements anyway.

If you want to inject a bit of humor into your speech, that's fine, but stick to just a couple of one-liners rather than long-winded jokes that lose the audience's attention before you've got to the punch line. It's probably more acceptable to tease your son than it is for the father of his bride to tease his daughter, but you will still want to be careful, particularly if he is easily embarrassed. It should be the day of his life; he doesn't want to look back on it thinking that everyone was laughing at him. If in any doubt, speak to your wife and possibly your son to check that you aren't saying anything out of order.

Thanks to the in-laws and others

It will be a nice touch to say thank you to your new in-laws. If they have footed much of the bill, you'll want to thank them for helping to arrange such a spectacular day. Avoid mentioning money though. If that isn't necessary, thanking them for bringing up such a lovely daughter will be much appreciated. You may not know your in-laws very well, in which case your words will hopefully help cement a long-lasting and fruitful relationship. Make sure that you have their names written down on prompt cards, especially if they are hard to pronounce, so that you don't get them wrong! If you do know them well, your words should ensure that your relationship continues to be a positive one.

If there are other people that you need to thank, do so after the in-laws. This may also be a good time to remind people of any important family members who are unable to attend.

Closing Remarks

Depending on how many speeches are still to be given, you may want to avoid giving a toast. Talk to your son and daughter-in-law about this. If you are under time pressure, giving a toast may be too time-consuming and guests may get sick of standing up and toasting the bride and groom more than a couple of times. You could simply say that you are now going to hand over to the next speaker, who could be your wife, or the groom himself.

If you do decide to give a toast, keep it as simple as possible by just turning to the bride and groom and asking everyone to raise a glass for their future happiness.

Giving a father of the groom speech may seem unnecessary and be a repetition of what has already been said. If you have strong feelings about giving one, or not giving one, you should discuss it with the bride and groom in advance so that there aren't any surprises on the day. If the wedding is very formal, or you have contributed a great deal towards the cost of the wedding, it may be only right for you to give a speech; otherwise, it really depends on how you all feel.

If you do decide to go ahead, you should practice your speech in advance in front of someone so that they can tell you whether anything you are planning to say is inappropriate and they can time you. Take prompt cards to refer to while giving the speech so that you don't end up stuttering your way through, thereby wasting valuable time. Don't run the risk of going over time because it won't be appreciated, especially if there are still several speeches to go.

Chapter 8: Examples of Father of the Groom Speeches

You will find that there are fewer examples of father of the groom speeches available online, or in any other source, simply because most people presume it will be the father of the bride who gives the main speech. That doesn't matter, because you can always look at father of the bride speeches and adapt them to suit. Your speech shouldn't be lifted directly from another source anyway, because you will want to inject plenty of your own personality.

You may think that your speech is not as important as some of the others, especially compared to the father of the bride, the bride and groom themselves and the best man, but you should still take the time to prepare what you are going to say.

Some ideas of how to start each stage of your speech are given below. You are then free to adapt them, or completely change them as necessary.

Introductions

"Good evening, all. I am X, the father of the groom for those of you who are wondering who I am. You'll be pleased to know that I will be keeping this speech short, but I do have a few things I want to say."

"I'm so pleased to see all the family members and friends who have taken the time to come here today to X and X's wedding. For those who don't know me, I am X's father, and this is his mother, X. We couldn't be prouder of X and X than we are today."

"Following the father of the bride's excellent speech, I'm going to keep this relatively brief because I know you all want to eat. As father of the groom, I do, however, want to thank you all for your presence today."

Anecdotes about your son

"I remember how proud I was when X was five and told me he wanted to be a brain surgeon. He didn't quite follow through there. However, he was the first of the family to get a degree and he's carried on achieving ever since. We couldn't be prouder of him."

"We were so pleased when X came home for dinner one day and told us that he had met 'the one' – that is, of course, the bride in case you were wondering. We were even more pleased when we met 'the one' and found out that she didn't have purple hair, nose rings or tattoos over every part of her body like some of his previous choices."

"It's never really been in my son's life plan to get married. He always wanted a great career, fast cars and a bachelor lifestyle.

Things changed the day he met X and I couldn't be happier for him – he's found a woman to tame him in the way that my wife tamed me. I'm sure she'll be happy to share some tips with the bride to make sure he stays that way!"

Thanks to the in-laws and others

"I want to especially thank X and X for having raised such a wonderful daughter and for letting her marry our son. They have done a great job and we look forward to getting to know them better over the coming years."

"The father of the bride has already thanked most of the people who needed thanking, but I would just like to mention one other person who helped make this day special. X has been a family friend for years and, as soon as she heard that X and X were planning to set their wedding date, she immediately offered to arrange all the flowers you've seen today as part of their wedding present. As you can see, she's done a fantastic job, so please join me in thanking her for her hard work."

"I can't let this opportunity slip by without mentioning my mother, X's grandmother, who is unable to be with us today. As some of you know, she recently had a stroke and, although she only lives a couple of hours' drive away, her doctor wouldn't let her travel to join us today. She is deeply disappointed, but is looking forward to seeing us all tomorrow when we visit her before X and X go off on their honeymoon."

Closing remarks

(If you've decided to give a toast) "Can I ask you all to stand once again and raise your glasses to the bride and groom?"

"I'm going to stop now because there are other people who want to say a few words. I'd just like to say again, on behalf of my wife and I, how pleased we are that you could all be here today to celebrate X and X's wedding."

"I'm going to bring this speech to a close before you get bored of me and introduce you to someone who will do a much better job, my wife, X."

The key to giving a successful speech as father of the groom is not to repeat what has already been said which will probably involve comparing notes with others beforehand, and to keep things as short as possible. Then you'll have the opportunity to say how proud you are of your son and his new bride without boring anyone.

Chapter 9: Tips for Mother of the Groom Speeches

As the mother of the groom, you'll be thrilled to be watching your son give his vows to the lady of his choice. It isn't tradition for the mother of the groom to give a speech, but if the mother of the bride has given a speech, or your son's father is not around to give one, it will be a great way of giving a touching tribute to your son.

Speak to your son about your thoughts and check that he and the bride are happy for you to give a speech along with everyone else. Generally, they should welcome your willingness to say a few words. Of course, if you have funded a large part of the wedding event, it will be expected that you will give a speech anyway; you may even be the first speaker.

As with all speeches, you should prepare what you want to say in advance. Even if you are a really confident person and think that you can get away without preparation, you may find that, on the day, you are so moved by the proceedings that you forget everything that you wanted to say.

Ask your son and fiancée for their views on how long they want you to speak. It is unlikely to be more than a couple of minutes, particularly if there are a number of other speakers. In any case, you want to deliver your speech without losing the audience's attention. Keep it to just a few minutes, perhaps finishing with a couple of one-liners before giving the toast, if you decide that you are going to take the plunge.

Introductions

You may already have been introduced to the wedding guests by the father of the groom, or the master of ceremonies. However, it's still a nice touch to introduce yourself and say how pleased you are to see everyone at the wedding. If you have close relations from your side of the family (rather than the father of the groom's), you may want to pay particular attention to them, especially if they've come a long way.

You may also want to pay homage to any close family members who weren't able to attend, either because of distance, illness, or even death. Those who couldn't attend will be touched to know that you remembered them on your son's big day and your son will almost certainly appreciate the mention of any relatives who are no longer alive.

Memories of your Son

Even if the father of the groom has already told a couple of stories about your son, you will have your own memories. It's a good idea to ask the father of the groom for an overview of what he is going to say, so that you can balance out your own words. For example, if his speech is going to be humorous, you may want to balance it out by highlighting the more sensitive side of your son and making it a moving speech, rather than a funny one.

Don't, however, be tempted to talk for too long. Most of the wedding guests will already know how wonderful your son is and those who don't will have the chance to make their own minds up in due course. Keep the anecdotes to just a couple of lines and leave it at that.

You will be hugely proud of your son and will probably find yourself moved to tears at some point during the wedding. Try to avoid crying during your speech, however; if you feel that you may be about to cry, you may need to cut your speech short. Wedding guests won't mind a few breaks in the voice, but they will be embarrassed if you break down completely. Don't be tempted to calm yourself by drinking too much because it may make you even more emotional.

Impressions of his Bride

Hopefully, you'll already know the bride well enough to say something honest and touching about her. You could say how you knew she was right for your son the first day you met her. You could also be totally honest and say that you weren't sure at first, but over the months and years that you've known her, she's proved herself to be the right person and you're thrilled to welcome her into your family.

If you don't know her well, stick to the obvious, such as saying how beautiful she looks and that you are looking forward to getting to know her better over the coming years. That will be a great way of starting your relationship off on a really positive note

Reflections on Marriage

Provided that you have positive reflections on marriage to share with the wedding participants, you may want to say a few words on what you have learned. Of course, your son and daughter-in-law will need to find their own way, but hopefully, they will take on board life lessons that you have already learned. You should make this section thought-provoking; save the humor for other parts of the speech.

If you don't have positive reflections and are now divorced from the father of the groom, it's probably wise to avoid saying much. You could just mention that you are not a reliable role model provided that you make it light-hearted. The last place to bring up an acrimonious break-up is at your son's wedding. It will just leave you looking like a bitter woman. In fact, if you know you are likely to say something you shouldn't, it is advisable to decline giving a wedding speech at all.

Closing Lines

To finish off the speech, just say a few more words about the happy couple and toast them. If you're worried about repeating yourself, or saying something that others have already said, research a few proverbs or wise quotes on the Internet. That will be a great way of saying something with great meaning that others will remember long after your speech has ended.

If you're one of a long line of people giving speeches, you will probably be worried that your speech will be overwhelmed by others. However, if you prepare it carefully and keep to your time slot, there is no reason why people shouldn't thoroughly enjoy your speech, especially for the personal insight into your son. Just be careful that, if there have already been a few toasts before yours, you haven't had too much to drink. A mother of the groom giving a slurred speech will be memorable for all the wrong reasons.

Chapter 10. Examples of Mother of the Groom Speeches

When it comes to preparing and drafting your mother of the groom speech, you'll want to make it original, attention-grabbing and suitable for your personality. There is little point in taking a speech directly from the Internet because it won't flow properly and, if it doesn't sound like something you would say, those in the audience who know you well will know that you didn't write it yourself.

At the same time, there is no reason why you can't take ideas from other people's speeches to give you some inspiration. You can then weave your own personality into the speech by playing around with it and trying it out in front of other people to see what they think. That is a good way of checking that you are not going over your allotted time slot and that you aren't saying anything inappropriate.

You will want to decide whether you want your speech to be humorous or moving; that will really depend on your personality, the theme of the wedding and whether you think you can carry off a humorous speech. You will need a certain amount of confidence to do so; otherwise, your jokes could fall flat.

When you start drafting your speech, divide it up into sections and start to collect your thoughts together. You could use some of the following ideas.

Introductions

"As X explained, I am X, the mother of the groom, and I'd like to take this opportunity to welcome you all here today. I'm delighted that so many of you could attend this stunning wedding."

"Good evening everyone, I am X's mother and I'm so honored to be here today to witness the marriage of X and X. Obviously, I've known X for a lot longer, but the short time I've known X has convinced me that she is the perfect woman for him."

(If you've contributed the most towards the wedding) "As you look around you today, I'm sure that you'll realize that a lot of work has gone into preparing the venues for the wedding. I have to say that it was all worth it because it looks stunning. It's my great pleasure that you were all able to attend today to share my son's vows to his new wife against this beautiful backdrop."

Stories about your Son

"I'm so proud of X. As some of you will remember, he was painfully shy as a little boy. I was so worried that he would find life difficult as he grew older. I needn't have worried. As he matured, his confidence increased, and he has done so well in his studies and career."

"X grew up as the only male in our little family. He was teased mercilessly by his two older sisters, but as the 'man of the house,' he always rose to the occasion when he was needed. It was a heavy burden to put on his young shoulders, but it has prepared him well for adulthood and marriage."

"X has come a long way since the time he announced at his cousin's wedding that he would never be getting married. He said he was going to stay home and look after me forever. But don't worry, X (bride's name), he was only five at the time!"

Impressions of the Bride

"X looks stunning today, doesn't she? I've known her for a long time now and have always thought she was beautiful, but today she looks positively radiant. And I can honestly say that she is beautiful both inside and out."

"As X lives so far away now, I've not had the chance to get to known X (the bride) as well as I would like. Yet it's obvious from what I do know that she is a confident, mature woman who is absolutely right for my son. She'll soon have all his weak points ironed out!"

"I've looked forward to the weddings of all my children even since they were born. X was always my baby and is the last to get married. I've been lucky in that all my children have married well and X is no exception. X (the bride) is one of the calmest, most even-tempered people I have ever met and will undoubtedly be able to keep X on the straight and narrow in their marriage."

Views on Marriage

"I've had a long and happy marriage to X's father and have been thinking about advice I can pass on to X and X. The most important thing is the willingness to talk things through. If there's a problem, don't ignore it, because it will fester and cause greater problems down the line. But I'm sure X and X already knows this."

"Those of you who know me will remember that I've been married and divorced three times. You may think I'm not the best person to be offering advice on marriage, but I'm going to give some anyway. Save time for each other. By all means work hard, but don't let work get in the way of your marriage. It is the most important thing you will ever have, so treasure it."

"People seem to walk into marriage so lightly these days. I know that X and X have taken the time to get to know each other first and that will prepare them well. But (turning to the bride and groom) marriage is hard work. There will probably be times when you wonder if you've made a mistake. It won't always be honeymoon and roses. Don't give up though. Talk to each other, be honest and don't sleep on an argument."

Ending the Speech

"Thank you all once again for coming today. Let's toast the bride and groom."

"Once again, I'm so happy that you could all come today to share in our happiness. Let's raise our glasses for X and X and wish them every happiness."

"X (your son), you have made an excellent choice of bride. Make sure you treat her with the respect she deserves. Remember that the more you invest in a marriage, the more valuable it becomes."

Research, draft and practice your speech so that you are confident about what you have to say. On the day itself, stand tall, look people in the eye and only refer to your notes when necessary. Then you can be sure of giving an Oscar-worthy performance.

Chapter 11. Tips for Speeches by the Groom

As the groom, you'll almost certainly be expected to give a short speech following the father (and possibly mother) of the bride and your own father (and possibly mother). As one of the two most important people at the wedding, everyone will want to hear from you, especially those who don't already know you very well, and you will probably have a few people whom you want to thank. If you're a very nervous public speaker, you should prepare in plenty of time and then practice in front of others so that you can be word perfect on your big day.

Whether you're a good public speaker or not, you should probably choose to keep the speech brief and to the point. People will be getting hungry and will be looking forward to having something to eat. Decide on a timeframe with your bride and stick to it. However, there are still a few key things that you should try to fit in. Use prompt cards to ensure that you don't leave anything out.

Introductions

You shouldn't need to introduce yourself, because everyone will know who you are. However, it's worth thanking everyone for taking the time to come to your wedding. This is a good time to thank those who had to travel a substantial distance to attend your big day, but it's also worth thanking your parents and your bride's parents for their contributions towards the wedding, whether financial or otherwise. If there are any other members of your family who deserve a mention and that haven't already been mentioned by your father, refer to them as well.

Talk about your Bride

You can't really give a speech as the groom and not mention your new wife! You will have already given your vows, so you don't need to say too much, but make what you say sincere. You could tell her that you could not believe your luck when she agreed to go out with you and that you cannot believe that she is now your wife. Tell her how much you love her and are looking forward to spending the rest of your life with her.

You could also share a couple of anecdotes about how you first met, particularly if there is something humorous you could share with the wedding guests, but keep it short and sweet.

Thank her Parents

In these modern times, it probably won't be necessary to thank your father-in-law for giving his daughter's hand in marriage, but it will still be a nice touch if you thank your in-laws for raising such a lovely daughter. You could mention how pleased you are that you are now all part of one family and that you are looking forward to spending many happy times with them over the coming years.

Thank the Best Man

Next, you should mention your best man and how he has been responsible for keeping you calm in the run-up to the wedding. You chose your best man for a reason, so tell everyone about him – perhaps he has been your best friend since childhood, or maybe he was a particularly good friend to you during a difficult time in your life. He will appreciate your candor.

Don't forget to mention his role in arranging the bachelor party either and thank him for keeping you out of trouble!

Mention the Bridesmaids and Groomsmen

Just as the best man supported you, the maid of honor and/or bridesmaids will have helped keep your bride calm in the build-up to the wedding. You may not be entirely familiar with what their roles were, so check with your bride in advance and pick one or two important contributions that they made to the success of the wedding. This could be arranging the bridal shower, choosing the wedding dress or helping to decorate the reception venue.

If you also had groomsmen, flower girls and page boys at your wedding, you will want to thank them too, unless, of course, your wife is also planning to make a speech and you would rather leave that to her. In that case, just make sure that you both discuss your speeches beforehand and make a checklist of who each of you will be thanking. Write the names down on prompt cards to have with you while giving your speech. You don't want to get to the end of the speech and then realize that you have missed out a key person.

Closing Remarks and Toast

You may want to close your speech by explaining to everyone what is going to happen for the rest of the evening. That will probably be a meal followed by entertainment, so let people know what time the entertainment is going to start. You may also want to mention where people who have brought wedding presents with them should put them.

End your speech by asking everyone to toast your bride and, if there is no master of ceremonies, introduce the next speaker.

If you're not someone who loves the limelight, your wedding day can be a very nerve-wracking experience because all eyes are on you. You could avoid giving a speech at all, particularly if you are having a very informal wedding, but it is probably best to make an effort to say a few words. In order to avoid panicking and stuttering your way through your speech, make sure you prepare what you want to say in advance and have bullet points written down on prompt cards. Don't, however, be tempted to write the whole speech out and read from it.

On the other hand, if you are a naturally confident person who is used to public speaking, don't be tempted to just stand up and say whatever comes to you. You may be surprised at how nervous you feel on your wedding day and it will certainly be overwhelming at times. Prepare a couple of weeks in advance and, as above, make sure you have prompt cards with you so that you ensure you thank everyone you need to.

Chapter 12. Examples of Speeches by the Groom

Your speech as the groom will probably be one of the most anticipated. Those who don't already know you will want to hear what you have to say and decide if they think you are right for the bride. Those who do know you will want to see some of your personality shine through. Of course, you won't necessarily be able to meet everyone's expectations, and you shouldn't make that a major source of concern, but you should be able to give a speech that will satisfy the majority of people.

There is, however, no need to worry because provided that you think through what you want to say and practice it in advance, there's no reason why you shouldn't give a speech to remember. This chapter provides some ideas for starting each section of your speech, after which you can inject your own personality to make the speech your own.

Introductions

"X and I are so pleased that you could all come to share our special day. From the moment we decided to get married, we knew that we wanted all of you to be with us."

"Thank you X for the introduction. Hopefully most of you already know who I am by now, but in case you don't, I'm X, now better known as X's husband!"

"Thank you all so much for coming today. X and I are thrilled to see you all here. I'd like to take this opportunity to thank four special people, without whom this wedding would never have happened. X and X, the mother and father of the bride, and my own mother and father have worked tirelessly over the last few months to help us realize our dream wedding. We want to thank them from the bottom of our hearts."

All about the Bride

"I think you'll all agree that X looks absolutely beautiful today. In my eyes, she always looks beautiful. Before I met her, I didn't believe in love at first sight. I was way too cynical. Then I went to X's wedding and, as soon as our eyes met, I knew she was the one for me."

"It's funny how opposites attract sometimes. As those of you who know me will know, I'm the confident, fun-loving, adventurous type, whereas X is much more introverted. Yet somehow we work together. She stops me from taking stupid risks and I've encouraged her to try parachuting! She's even better at it than me!"

"I remember the first time X met my best friends, including X, the best man here. They were bowled over by her looks, but more than that, by the time they'd been with her for a couple of hours, they were bowled over by her personality too.

They're still telling me they don't know how I managed to get her to marry me!"

Thanks to other members of the wedding party

"As well as thanking the bride's parents for their role in organizing the magnificent event you see before you, I want to thank them for raising such a beautiful, kind and caring daughter. I knew before I met them that they must be amazing people because otherwise they couldn't have produced such a wonderful daughter."

"When I asked X to be my best man, I think he was a bit overwhelmed. He certainly spilled his beer all over the place – and this is a man who doesn't waste his beer for anything! Seriously though, he has been an amazing choice. Much as I've looked forward to marrying X, I was really nervous about standing up today in front of you all. I even doubted whether she would turn up! But X (best man) has done everything he can to keep me calm. Most importantly, he made sure I got here today in plenty of time!"

"Just as I need to thank X for being my best man, I also want to mention the groomsmen, who have also played a role in keeping me calm and helped direct all the guests to their seats. I'm sure you'll agree they did a great job."

"I also want to thank X, the maid of honor, for fulfilling the same role as X (the best man). Well, okay, it wasn't quite the same role. The best man didn't have to accompany me to try on wedding dresses! All joking aside though, she's done a great job and I want her to know how grateful I am."

"Last but not least, I want to thank X, X and X, the bridesmaids, for looking so beautiful and for all their organizing skills, and also X, the flower girl and X, the ring bearer. Didn't they do an amazing job? I look forward to attending their weddings in due course."

How to Close

"Before I pass you on to X, I'd like you all to toast my beautiful wife and all those just mentioned for helping make our day so very beautiful."

"Please all raise your glasses to toast X."

"Thank you all again for being part of our wedding. Let's raise a glass to celebrate our union."

When you look back over your life in years to come, your wedding day will hopefully be one of the highlights. Of course, it will be the fact that you married the love of the life that you will remember the most, but if you gave a great speech, you will also be look back with the satisfaction of knowing that you played an important part in a wonderful day.

Chapter 13. Tips for Speeches for the Bride

By convention, the bride doesn't give a speech; that honor is left to the father of the bride, the groom, and the best man and possibly the father of the groom. However, in this day and age, women are supposed to be men's equals, so if you want to give a speech, there is no reason why you shouldn't! You may also want to encourage the other women in your bridal party to say a few words to even out the balance. If you're a real feminist, or you just think that women have played a more important part in the organization of your wedding than the men, you may just want the women to speak!

People will probably be looking forward to hearing from you, especially if they know that you are likely to give a confident, polished speech. Just bear in mind that you still need to prepare in advance, even if you're only planning on speaking for a couple of minutes. You'll probably want to thank a long list of people and the last thing you want to do is miss anyone out. Take prompt cards with you on the day, or at least a sheet of paper with a bullet points, so that you don't miss anyone out.

It's your big day. You can more or less say anything you want. However, you may still want to err on the side of caution. You may have a sarcastic sense of humor that everyone who knows you well will understand, but that quirkiness could be misinterpreted as over-confidence and you don't want to start your married life having fallen out with half of your new husband's family. At the very least, tone it down a little and ask someone for feedback on your speech before you decide on the final version.

It's a good idea to compare notes with your husband-to-be before you sign off on what you want to say. Even if you both have a great sense of humor, you don't want to put each other in embarrassing positions and you will both know whether what you have to say is going to offend anyone else.

By splitting your speech up into sections, you can make sure that you say everything you want to say. The following sections will probably include a lot of what you want to say.

Introduction

Unless you are having a very small and intimate wedding and you are sure that everyone knows who you are, it's a good idea to introduce yourself! You may not have had time to meet all the groom's side of the family at this stage! You'll also want to thank everyone for coming and say that you hope they enjoy themselves.

Give thanks to your parents and those of the groom's, especially if they have played a big role in making the arrangements for the wedding. If the groom has already thanked them, just say a few words and move on. They'll appreciate the acknowledgement, but if you talk too long, you'll just bore everyone.

Anecdotes about your husband

You may not have known your husband for as long as his parents, but you will have a personal knowledge of him that no one else does. Choose a couple of stories that highlight why you love him. You can make these as funny or as serious as you like, but don't get too personal! No one wants to know the ins and outs of your sex life on your wedding day!

If you've had a whirlwind marriage, or have been together for years before getting married, you may want to make a few remarks about this. People will be interested in knowing the reasons behind your decision and this will help make your speech particularly memorable.

A few words about your in-laws

The mother and father of the groom are an important part of the wedding party, so don't neglect to say a few words directed at them. You could thank them for bringing up such a great son. You and your husband will have already thanked them for helping with the wedding arrangements, but you could also talk about ways that they have helped you in the past; perhaps you and your husband lived with them while you were saving money, or perhaps they lent you some money towards the deposit of a house.

Show that you appreciate the maid of honor and/or bridesmaids

Your husband will probably have already thanked the best man and possibly the rest of the immediate wedding party too. If he hasn't, of course, you will need to thank them, but otherwise, keep any mention of them to a minimum.

You will, however, want to thank your maid of honor and/or the bridesmaids. Make sure you let the rest of the wedding guests know how they have helped you. They will probably have helped organize the bridal shower and bachelorette party. They may have helped you choose your wedding dress and make the decorations for the reception. At the very least, they will have helped keep you calm in the few days before the wedding. They will probably have spent a lot of time and energy (and possibly money) helping you to organize your big day. Let everyone know how much you appreciate them.

At this stage in your speech, it is a good time to give out any thank you gifts you have for your mother, the mother of the groom and the maid of honor and bridesmaids. Then again, you may prefer to do this in private afterwards. It's your choice.

Final Words

You'll want to give a toast to everyone who has had an important role in making your special day so happy, but pay particular attention to the maid of honor and bridesmaids because other speakers probably won't have given them more than a passing mention. Then thank everyone for coming and introduce the next speaker.

In many ways, you could be a better choice to give a wedding speech than the groom. You will have been involved in the arrangements from start to finish and will know exactly how much work each individual has contributed. If you would prefer to give a speech in place of the groom, discuss it with him in plenty of time. He may well be relieved that you will be taking on the responsibility so that he can relax and enjoy the wedding reception.

Chapter 14. Examples of Speeches for the Bride

Once you've decided on the sections of your speech and know approximately what you want to say in each, it's time to start thinking about the actual wording. It's a good idea to do some research online to find out what other people have said, then you can adjust it as necessary so that it suits your temperament. Use the suggestions that follow in this chapter too. At the very least, you can decide on what you don't want to say.

Remember that this is hopefully the only time you are going to be making a wedding speech, so make it count! Practice in advance so that you are as well-rehearsed as possible. The more prepared you are, the more relaxed and able to enjoy yourself on your big day you will be.

Opening Lines

"I don't think anyone who knows me will be surprised that I have decided to break with tradition and give a wedding speech. Those who know me well will be surprised to find out in a minute or two that I'm only saying a few words!"

"Thank you for the wonderful words that my father and the groom's father have already said. I would like to reiterate how grateful X and I are that you have all come today. It wouldn't have been the same without you and we do hope that you enjoy yourselves."

"For those of you who don't know me yet, I'm X and it's great to see you all here. I can assure you that by the end of this evening, you'll feel like you know me well. I have that effect on people!"

Comments about the Groom

"In the time I've got, I don't know how I'm going to put into words how happy I am that I am now Mrs. X. Ever since I met him, X has been my rock. He's stuck with me throughout the good times and the bad times and there he is still beside me. I cannot wait to start our married life together."

"When X and I first met, it wasn't really love at first sight. In fact, we hated each other. He was a friend of a friend and I thought he was far too confident. He thought I was too domineering. But over the following months, we got to know each other and we both came to realize that we were a better fit than we thought. Now I can't imagine life without him and I know he feels the same way about me. He'd better do anyway!"

"So many people have commented on my hair, dress and makeup and I'm very grateful for all the great things they've said. I'd just like to say how wonderful X looks. In fact, I've never seen him looking so good! I hope he keeps this up for the rest of our lives together!"

Thanks to your Parents-in-Law

"I haven't had the chance to get to know X and X yet, but from what my husband has told me, I know we're going to have a great relationship! I'm looking forward to spending many happy days in California getting to know them better."

"I'd like to thank X and X for their support in all the time I've known them. They welcomed me into their home from the moment I met them and, although we come from different cultures, they have never once judged me or asked me to behave in a certain way."

"X and X, I'd like to thank you not just for all the help you have given in planning the wedding, but also for having brought up the kind and loving man whom I have just married. You've done such a good job and I'm so grateful."

Show gratitude for the maid of honor and bridesmaids

"They say diamonds are a girl's best friend. That's not true. X is my best friend and she's far more valuable to me than diamonds. She has stuck with me through thick and thin and, without her as maid of honor, I don't think I would have got through the last few days. X, you're wonderful. Thank you so much."

"I wouldn't be standing here today if it wasn't for these lovely ladies in burgundy. They've contributed so much towards this wedding, from helping me choose my dress, to sending out the invitations and making sure that everything went so smoothly today."

"Before I give a toast, I'd just like to give a big shout out to my maid of honor, X, for all her help with keeping me calm over the past few days, and also for letting me borrow her daughter, X, to be the flower girl. I'm sure you'll agree that they both looked wonderful."

Closing Lines and Toast

"I don't want to take up any more of your time, so please be on your feet, here's a toast to everyone who is here today – to love, laughter and friendship."

"You'll all be amazed, but that's it from me. All I want to do now is to toast my husband and the wedding party and to ask you all to enjoy yourselves for the rest of the evening!"

"Once again, thank you all for joining us on our big day. It wouldn't have been the same without you. Please all raise your glasses for a toast."

Let your personality shine through in your speech by being yourself, without causing anyone any offence. Don't forget that you'll be watching your wedding video after your wedding and you don't want to feel embarrassed by what you said. Fortunately, if you are as well-rehearsed as possible, there's no reason why you should be.

Chapter 15. Tips for Best Man Speeches

The best man's speech will usually come last; however, if the maid of honor or one of the bridesmaids is also giving a speech, you may be second to last. However, most people will be expecting you to give the speech of the evening, so you'll need to start preparing in plenty of time.

Before you start researching what to say, talk to the bride and groom and ask them what they are expecting from your speech. It's traditional for the best man speech to be a hilarious, riotous affair, but the bride and groom may not want that. You may also be concerned that giving a funny speech doesn't suit your character, in which case, you'll want to share your views and let them know that your speech won't be a laugh a minute. In that case, you might want to go for a speech that tugs at the heart strings instead.

On the other hand, you may be nervous because you think the bride and groom will expect you to be overly sentimental, whereas you are the joker of the pack. In that case, it's fine to aim to make everyone laugh; if you let the bride and groom know in advance, they can balance this out by asking someone else to give a more sentimental speech.

If you hate public speaking, you'll need to do plenty of preparation and practice so that you feel as confident as possible on the day of your speech. It's fine to say at the beginning of your speech that you are really nervous. You can turn it into a joke by saying that the groom forced you to become best man to punish you for a prank you played on him in the past. However, even if you love being at center stage, you'll still need to prepare well in advance. Several speeches may have been given before you get your chance and you don't want to waste more time because you've forgotten what you want to say.

Before we break your speech down into sections to help you decide what to say at each stage, remember to keep your speech as short as possible. People could be sick of speeches by your turn, so aim to speak for just a few minutes unless the bride and groom say otherwise. On the day, you may want to revise your speech even further by missing out an anecdote or two. Judge the audience's concentration levels just before you start speaking.

Explain how you know the Groom

By the time it is your turn to give a speech, the audience will be sick of hearing introductions, so keep yours short. It is probably enough to say that you are thrilled to have been asked to be best man and that the presence of so many people is testament to the personalities of the wonderful bride and groom.

Remember to introduce yourself by name, of course, because it's quite possible many people don't know who you are, particularly if you haven't known the groom for all that long. Say how you met the groom and why you were asked to be best man.

Give Thanks

Again, you will want to keep this section short because other speakers will already have expressed thanks to the majority of people who deserve it. Check in advance with the bride and groom if there is anyone else you should thank; otherwise, just stick to thanking the groomsmen and bridesmaids and leave it at that.

Talk about the Groom

This should be the main part of your speech. The guests will want to know a little bit more about the groom and this is the time to come up with a couple of funny stories if you can carry off humor. However, that doesn't mean that you should drag up every embarrassing story you can think of. Remember that there will be a mix of age groups at the wedding, including the very old and the very young, and you really don't want to say anything that will cause offence.

If you have a sarcastic sense of humor and are aware that not everyone understands it, run the stories by the bride and groom in advance. If they aren't happy with what you are planning to say, then don't say it.

If funny and entertaining is not your style, try and think of a couple of interesting and possibly sentimental stories about the groom and keep your speech as short as possible.

Praise the Bride and her Choice in Man

You'll hopefully know the bride quite well, in which case, you could share a story or two about how the bride and groom met and what happened when you met her for the first time. If you don't know her well, just say something about how she couldn't have made a better choice in husband and you know that they will both be happy for ever more.

At this stage, if you are married yourself, you may want to give some advice on the recipe for a successful marriage. If you're not married, steer clear of giving advice because you won't be taken seriously.

Closing Remarks and Toast

You'll be expected to give a toast to the bride and groom, so be prepared to do so. If you want to finish your speech off with laughter or something thought-provoking, you could search online to see if you can finding any good proverbs or sayings that share what you want to say. You may find that this is a less wordy way of getting your meaning across than finding your own words. Then give your toast and sit down, feeling confident that you have given an enjoyable speech.

Best man speeches are often the highlight of the more formal part of the wedding. This may make you feel as though you are under a lot of pressure. However, plenty of preparation should mean that you can deliver your speech successfully. Remember not to drink too much the night before, or at the wedding reception before you give your speech. Alcohol may give you some Dutch courage, but it may also help you to make a fool of yourself. Stay sober until after you've spoken.

Chapter 16. Examples of Best Man Speeches

You'll find many examples of best man speeches available online. The problem is more likely to be that you don't know where to start. The best way to get around this is to break the speech up into manageable chunks and then find examples that suit you and your personality.

This chapter will offer a few suggestions of how to break your speech up and then how to introduce each chunk. Once you've done this, you can play around with the words, feeding in your own personal stories, until you come up with something that sounds like your own words. Take your time with this. You may be dreading giving a speech, but leaving it until the night before the wedding really isn't a good idea.

Explain your Relationship to the Groom

"I know you're all hungry, so don't worry, this will be short. I'm sure some of you will be wondering how I know X. Well, we've been lifelong friends. I know all his embarrassing stories. But don't worry, X (groom's name), I'll only have time to share a couple. If the rest of you want to know any more, come and see me afterwards!"

"I've only been a friend of X's for the past couple of years. We met when we worked on a project in Cancun and we've been great friends ever since. I look forward to getting to know those I haven't met during the rest of the evening."

"I'm not a great public speaker and I'm really nervous, but when X asked me to be his best man, I just couldn't turn the opportunity down. He's the best friend I have and I hope that I can do him justice this evening."

Thanks to the Wedding Party

"You're probably bored of hearing never-ending thanks to different people involved in organizing the wedding, so I am going to keep this part short. I just need to say thanks to the bridesmaids who did a great job today in keeping the bride composed and for giving me advice on how to keep the groom calm!"

"I'd just like to say thanks to the bride and groom for inviting my son, X, to be the ring bearer today. I think you'll all agree he did a great job; after all, he managed to get the ring from the back of the church to me at the front without losing it on the way!"

"Thanks to everyone involved in organizing this wonderful event today. It's obvious that a huge amount of work has gone into it and I find it amazing that the bride and members of the wedding party have done most of it themselves. You should all be very proud of yourselves."

Share a Couple of Stories about the Groom

"X has come a long way since we first met at Risley High. Then he was determined to have as much fun as possible; forget about having a career. He's really pulled himself together since then. He really deserves everything he has now, including a beautiful bride!"

"One thing I've come to learn about X over the years is his loyalty. He has got me out of scrapes far more often than I would like. For that reason, I'm not going to tell you all the embarrassing stories about him you're probably expecting. I've got to repay him for his loyalty some time!"

"It's obvious why X and I are such good friends – we share one particular characteristic in that we're both lazy! We've always been the guys who stay at home to watch a movie with some beers rather than get dressed and go out. It's a miracle we managed to make it here today! Don't we both look great? Take a good look because it will probably never happen again!"

Talk about the Bride and her Relationship with the Groom

"I honestly couldn't believe it when X told me he'd met the love of his life. He was always a 'love them and leave them' sort of guy. I remember when he was with his previous girlfriend. Lovely woman, but she hated letting him out of her sight, even when it was to meet me. Now he's met X, I can see that she is the right person for him. She trusts him implicitly, for good reason, and, most importantly, she doesn't mind when we go off to Vegas for the weekend!"

"When I first met X, I couldn't believe she wanted to be with my best friend. As you can see, she's gorgeous and he's just an ordinary guy, like me. Getting to know her has made me realize just how gorgeous she is inside too. I have no doubt that she will make X very happy and I want her to know that I will do my best to keep him on the straight and narrow. X, just send him my way if he misbehaves and I will sort him out for you!"

Closing Remarks

"You'll all be getting hungry, so that's enough from me. I'd just like you all to stand up to give one last toast to the happy couple!"

"Don't worry, the speeches are almost over; there's just one more after this. Let's just make a toast to the bride and groom and the rest of the wedding party and thank you all once again for joining us today."

"Without any more fuss, let's make a final toast to Mr. and Mrs. X. May your married life be the happiest possible."

Rehearse your best man speech as much as you can beforehand. Then you should be able to have fun, even if you are a little nervous.

Chapter 17. Tips for Maid of Honor or Bridesmaid Speeches

It's becoming more popular for the maid of honor or one of the bridesmaids to give a speech at the wedding reception. If the bride asks you to speak, or you really want to, there's no reason why you shouldn't. You may, however, want to check how many other people are going to be speaking before you make your final decision. You could be the last of eight, by which time you will need a great deal of personality to keep everyone's attention.

If you do decide to give a speech, another thing to consider is what you are going to say. The previous speakers will have already thanked everyone that should be thanked and there will probably have already been a number of stories told about the bride and groom. Really, you should have something different to add, otherwise, there is not much point in speaking.

On the other hand, if you're a confident public speaker, you could end the speeches on a high note with your humorous speech and, if there aren't many other female speakers, you will make a refreshing change.

You will probably be able to give a different take from the other speeches because of your familiarity with the bride. Make sure that your anecdotes are funny rather than offensive though. Your speech will be heard by a lot of people, including the bride's close family. There are some things that they just won't want to hear.

You probably won't find many examples of maid of honor speeches on the Internet because it's still a relatively uncommon occurrence. However, there's no reason why you can't take some of the suggestions in the following chapter and customize them to make them your own. Provided you give yourself plenty of time to prepare, you'll probably find it's easier than you thought to put your speech together.

Keep the Introductions to a Sentence or Two

The wedding guests will be tired by this time won't want to sit through another long introduction. Just tell people who you are and how you know the bride. Then move on.

Give General Thanks to the Wedding Party

This is another section that should be kept very short because the guests will already have heard about who contributed the most towards the wedding arrangements. Just thank the wedding party in general for their time and energy and get on to the core of your speech.

Share a Couple of Stories about the Bride

This is really where you will have the chance to shine. People will want to know about the bride when she was younger and before she was ready to start her married life as a mature woman. If you've known her since you were at school together, that is even better. Come up with a few stories of your time together. If you get stuck, asking other friends for their contributions can be helpful.

Bear in mind that you want to choose stories that are funny, but not ones that are offensive. A wedding isn't the time to be too over the top; you will be better off sticking to stories that are light-hearted and show your friend in the best possible light. Keep the stories about her being too drunk to walk home after she broke up with her first boyfriend to yourself.

Say Something about the Groom

Your knowledge about the groom and his relationship with the bride will also be of interest to the wedding guests. You will probably have seen a different side to their relationship than the one their parents see, so it will be a refreshing change to have a third party's take on it. Try to say something funny without being rude.

You could talk about how the couple first met and your first impressions of the bridegroom. You could also share the story of the wedding proposal.

If you don't know the groom very well, perhaps because your friend has lived elsewhere since she has known him, just keep your comments very brief. You could say that you know the groom is very worthy of your friend and that you don't doubt he will look after her well.

Just make sure that you focus on the positives. If you are jealous that your friend is getting married and you aren't, or you can't stand the groom and you don't think you can hide it in your speech, it will be much more sensible if you avoid making a speech at all. This is your best friend's day, and it should be all about her, not you.

Concluding Remarks

After your short speech, it is up to you whether you give yet another toast. You may prefer to simply say that you hope your friend and her husband will be very happy, that you are the last speaker and that you hope everyone enjoys their meals. That should be the signal to the waiters that it is time to start bringing the food out.

As the final speaker, you'll want to make sure you end on a high note, rather than be faced with a room full of bored guests. Provided that you take time to plan you speech, there is every reason why you should be able to keep their attention for the duration of your speech.

Chapter 18. Examples of Maid of Honor/Bridesmaid Speeches

What you choose to say during your speech should be very personal to you and the bride. However, that doesn't mean you can't seek inspiration from the Internet and from the ideas in this chapter. You can then work your personality around them to give a humorous and entertaining speech.

Remember not to get carried away and prepare a speech that takes too long. If the bride doesn't give you a timeframe, aim to speak for no longer than three to four minutes; ideally less than that. Practice and time yourself so that you don't go over.

Check with the bride whether there is anything she particularly wants you to say. She may, for example, want you to thank particular people if you know them better than any of the other speakers. Otherwise, just stick to thanking people in general and quickly move on to the personal stories you have planned.

Dividing your speech up into manageable chunks should help keep you focused as you do your preparation and will help you to remember everything you want to say. However, it is still advisable to have prompt cards with you on the day.

Introducing Yourself

"Some of you won't know me, so to quickly introduce myself, I'm X and I'm the maid of honor. I was delighted to be asked to take on this role because I've known X since we were five years old and sat next to each other at school."

"Thanks to the best man for that amazing speech. As he said, I am X, one of the bridesmaids, and I've known X since we shared a dorm room at college."

"I know you're all getting bored now, so I'm going to keep this speech short. I just wanted to say a few words as the maid of honor."

Thanks to the Wedding Party

"I think it's obvious that a great deal of hard work has gone into getting the wedding venue ready today. It's taken months of planning. I'd like to thank everyone involved for what they've achieved because they've obviously done an amazing job."

"The bride thanked me earlier for helping her stay calm over the past few weeks. But compared to the productivity of many of the other people you see here on the head table, I'm almost too embarrassed to accept her thanks. (Turning to the others at the head table) You've all done such a beautiful job, I'm overwhelmed."

"I am so touched to have been invited to be one of X's bridesmaids. It really is a huge honor. X, thank you so much for the opportunity."

Stories about the Bride

"I've known the bride for many years now and I've seen her in quite a few relationships over the years. But she was never really happy until she met X. It was obvious when she was with him that she felt completely relaxed. I've never seen her like that. It was obvious right from the start that their relationship was a match made in heaven. I only hope that I meet my perfect match one day like they have."

"When I look back over the years since I've known X, it's hard to believe that the scruffy little tomboy who liked nothing better than climbing trees and searching for birds' eggs is the same person who's sat here today looking like a princess. But she doesn't just look like a princess; she really is a princess. She's the best friend I've ever had and I know we'll be best friends for life.

"I haven't really known X all that long. We met through work because we shared the same kitchen. We started off by complaining about our jobs, but then realized we had so much more in common that work and became inseparable. When I needed somewhere to live after a relationship ended, she suggested I moved in with her. Now she's getting married, I'm sad that we won't be living together any more, but I know I'll be a regular visitor to the home she now shares with X."

Comments on the Groom

"As I've already said, it was obvious that X and X were a perfect fit. I met him after they'd had a couple of dates because X wanted to know what I thought of him. Straight away I told her that he was a keeper. He treats her with respect and that is a rare commodity in this day and age."

"I haven't had the chance to get to know X as much as I would like, but it's enough for me that X has chosen him as her life partner. She's always had great taste; she chose me as her best friend, after all!"

"I've known X for almost as long as I've known the bride; they came as a package. I cannot imagine one without the other. I have never seen a better matched couple and I have no doubt that they will live happily ever after."

Closing Remarks and Toast

"Let's raise our glasses for one last toast – to the bride and groom!"

"X and X, I wish you every happiness for your married life. Here's hoping we all have futures as bright and shiny as yours."

"For one last time before the meal begins, let's hear it for the bride and groom!"

Your speech will almost certainly be the final one, so ensure you make your mark by coming up with something pithy, funny and sensitive. It will be much appreciated.

Afterword (Conclusion)

Thank you for downloading this e-book; we hope you have found it useful, no matter what your role at the wedding. To summarize, here is a checklist of things that you should remember whether you are giving the first or last speech, or are somewhere in the middle:

Research

Everyone will tell you that you have to speak from the heart and that is very true. However, that doesn't mean you have to sit at home for days on end trying to find inspiration. If you're short of creativity, there is nothing wrong with doing some research online or using other sources, such as this e-book, and then customizing it to fit your own personality. Just make sure that you don't lift whole chunks that don't sound anything like something you would say.

Practice

You need to practice, whether you are a good public speaker or not. Last-minute nerves can take over otherwise. Stand in front of the mirror and check what you look like as you speak. Look straight into your own eyes and check your body language. If you are hunched over, make an effort to stand up straight. If you plan to take prompt cards with you, bring them up to chest level rather than bend over and hide your face.

Ask Advice

It's a really good idea to ask other people to listen to your speech. They can then tell you if anything isn't appropriate, or it doesn't flow well. Even if you're the bride, you don't want to say anything that will offend any of the wedding guests.

This could be particularly important if the bride and groom come from different cultures. What could be perfectly acceptable in one culture may be a real no-no in another. Don't presume that everyone has become Americanized because that may not be the case.

Keep to your Time Limit

You should really discuss the time limit with the bride and groom in advance. If they don't have a firm idea, aim to speak for no more than five minutes. You may want to have a couple of sections that you can miss out if you think that the wedding guests are getting bored. On the day, keep an eye on the guests while others are speaking and gauge whether they are becoming restless.

Don't Memorize

If you're not a good public speaker, you may be tempted to write your entire speech out and memorize it until you are word perfect. This is not a good idea. You then run the risk of going blank when you get up to do your speech. It doesn't look good if you then have to pick up several sheets of paper and look through them to find the bit you want. Even if you do manage to memorize your speech and get through it without a mistake on the day, you are likely to sound like an automaton.

It is much more advisable to have a few prompt cards with bullet points so that you can talk around them. If you practice enough in advance, you should be able to do this without any problem.

Decide Whether to Give a Toast in Advance

If there are only a couple of people giving speeches, there is no reason why each of them can't give a toast. However, if there's a string of eight people giving toasts, wedding guests are going to get bored and the speeches will seem lackluster. There are a couple of people who should give toasts, including the first speaker, the bride and groom and the best man, but the others can probably get away without giving a toast. Make sure this is all discussed in advance so that everyone who is speaking knows what to expect.

Be confident

Confidence is not easy to exude if you aren't a very confident person. However, remember that it is just a few minutes of your life. If you know you are likely to be shaking with fear on the big day, try and find ways of relaxing. You may want to try different breathing techniques to make your voice sound confident even if you aren't feeling it. Standing straight and tall will do the same thing. Of course, practice will also help with your confidence levels.

Smile!

If you stand there looking nervous, you are going to make the wedding guests feel nervous too. By all means tell them that you are nervous, but do so with a smile. If you smile, they will smile back and you'll feel a whole lot better.

Remember that it is a great honor to be invited to give a wedding speech. But don't forget that it will all be over in a couple of minutes. Make those couple of minutes count and give a great speech that will be talked about for years to come.

If you enjoyed this book, then I'd like to ask you for a favor;
Would you be kind enough to
leave a review for this book on Amazon?
It'd be greatly appreciated!
Thank you and good luck!
Visit our website www.bestbuykindleebooksstore.com

FREEE BONUS OFFER!

Thanks again for purchasing the book
'**Wedding Speeches:**
A Practical Guide for Delivering an
Unforgettable Wedding Speech.' Included with this purchase is 1
FREE download of Ready-Made wedding speeches...Scroll down to
find out more.

BONUS+ OFFER

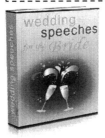

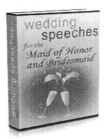

Related Books by Sam Siv

Below you'll find some of Sam Siv's related books that are popular on Amazon and Kindle as well. Simply click on the book pictures below to check them out.

Alternatively, you can also visit <u>Sam Siv's author page</u> on Amazon.com to see his other work as well.

 The number of weddings is on the rise, but these days, most couples don't have the time to plan this special day. This book was written to assist every bride and groom who needs to plan their big day by making a detailed checklist, including advice on transportation, locations, reception options, catering, protocol, photography, guest services, the dress, the groom's tux, the rings, the gifts, the cake, the best man and maid of honor, and ultimately, the wedding ceremony it-self. Your special day does not have to be a nerve-wracking experience, even if you have a number of people whom you want to invite. It is the most important day of your life, after all, and you will want everything to be perfect.

This book contains proven steps and strategies to planning your wedding from ring selection and the expectations of family and friends, which should be your first priority before any other planning begins. The content in this book has also been written to reflect the most current wedding tips and advice, etiquette, ideas to personalize the wedding, how to set budget parameters outlining whom will be paying for what, and how to create guest lists for seating, organize the catering, and further planning. In additional, this handy book also includes a checklist of things to do, detailed budget analysis, wedding party responsibilities, paying the vendors and other useful advice and tips. By keeping an eye on your budget as you go along,

When you're organizing a wedding, there are many points of etiquette that should be considered. Even if you're not usually the type of person to follow etiquette and guidelines, it's important that, for your wedding, you bear in mind that it is not just you who needs to be happy with the event – you want your family and other guests to enjoy the day too. By conforming to etiquette, you can ensure that everyone has an assigned role and knows what they are doing on your big day so that the event goes as smoothly as possible.

"Wedding Etiquette Guide: An Essential Guide Book For The Most Memorable Wedding Celebration" will look at the different points of etiquette that you should follow, beginning from the time that you get engaged, right through to sending out thank-you notes after you return from your honeymoon. It will provide a breakdown of who should be responsible for which duties in the planning stages of the wedding, as well as on the big day itself. It will also look at what happens in the unlikely event that you need to call off your wedding at the last minute because your relationship does not work out.

Once you have read this book, you will have a much better idea of what you should and shouldn't be doing in the preparations for your wedding. Of course, that doesn't mean that you don't have any control over the way that your wedding is held, but it does give you a foundation on which you can base your wedding planning and will ensure that all your guests are left with fond memories of a happy day spent with loved ones.
Use this book as a checklist at each stage of your wedding planning and, before long, you will be looking forward to your wedding day knowing that you have done everything you can to make it the best day of your life.

Readers will know how to shop for the perfect wedding dress for them.
A wedding dress is not just any dress. A wedding dress is THE dress of a lifetime. That's why it is so important to choose just the right one for you.

Upon reading this book, brides will be better equipped to shop for their wedding dress by:

*Knowing the different styles of wedding dresses they have to choose from
*Understanding which dresses look best on their body shape
*Knowing what styles of dresses are appropriate for the wedding they are planning
*Discovering different options for purchasing a wedding dress
*Pictures of dresses/gowns...and more pictures...for inspirations!
*Much, much more!

When the "I do's" have been said and you are on your way to happily ever after, you will be able to look back on your wedding day and know without a doubt that you looked as beautiful on the outside as you felt on the inside on your wedding day.

Reviews:

Beautifully inspired creation by Tricia Johnson

Wedding Dresses - Special Dresses for that Special Day by Christie Davis

You're about to discover proven steps on how to discover inspiration and ideas for your special day.

This book contains proven steps and strategies that will help you choose the perfect hair style for your wedding! As a bride, you need to look flawless on your special day. This book will help you choose the most appropriate look as you walk down the aisle. Whether you want something traditional or something shocking, there is something for you to learn in the pages of this book. What are the things you need to decide on? How will you choose your stylist? What accessories do you need? The answers you are looking for are in this book! It has everything you need to look and feel fabulous on your most special day.

Reviews:

An Excellent Guide to Wedding Hairstyles by Karsun

This book is awesome. It is simple and very adaptable by Micha

The perfect guide for brides on their big day.

Your wedding is one of the most important events of your life, the day of dreams and fantasies. This is the one true day you get to be the princess you are. To make this happen in a beautiful and tasteful way we have created the perfect guide to steer you in the right direction with the selection of your Center Piece. Get yourself a cool drink or warm beverage, put your feet up and prepare to be enchanted.

Reviews:

Valuable Information on Flower Arrangements by Vanessa D.

It provides some great photographs as examples by Cynthia Wall

You're about to discover inspirations and ideas for your special day.

This book contains steps and strategies that will help you choose the perfect cake for your wedding!

With the help of this book, you will be able to understand the traditions and symbolism which can help you in picking the cake you want.

We want you to have a perfect wedding, and we want to help you choose the perfect cake.

Whether you want something traditional or something quirky, you will surely find something inspiring in the pages of this book.

Reviews:

Took With Me to The Baker and Got My Dream Wedding Cake by Vanessa D.

I'm amazed by the creativity of the cakes illustrated in this book! By Claire

Readers will discover the numerous benefits of meditation; many of which are often overlooked and underused.

Life is stressful, but it doesn't have to be. That's right! You can actually enjoy a life virtually unaffected by stress and tension. How? Through the practices of meditation and relaxation, that's how. Readers of Meditation for Everyday Living will discover how to live a happy and successful life by spending twenty minutes a day in meditation.

Reviews:

Excellent Stress Reliever and Meditation Start-Up Guide By Vanessa D.

A must have meditation guide for everyday living By Cindy

Do you find yourself intimidated by different hard-bodied pretzel poses? Would you like to learn life-enhancing benefits of yoga? If your answer is yes, it time to start experiencing the many benefits of yoga. If you are someone who may have heard of yoga, but don't know how to begin your experience allow us to share various elements of yoga to a newcomer who may wonder whether yoga can help them.

Yoga is beginning to be more recognized now than ever as a great way to feel confident and to feel fulfilled in your life. If you are ready to start enjoying life enhancing benefits of yoga, this is a must read. Allow us to help your body build strength, increase flexibility and be a healthier you.

Yoga is available to everyone in this world today, and that includes you. You can learn Yoga regardless of your age, and physical condition and you can learn through the pages of this book, to become more balanced and have a more peaceful life.

Reviews:

What Yoga really is about By PookieThePirate

Highly recommended, especially to beginners like me. By Claire

There's a very good reason why this book was written. In a world where there are so many pressures, it was so clear to me that people no longer see the true choices which are available to them which allow them to be happy. Positive thinking isn't always as obvious to people as it should be. In fact, the pressures put on people to "excel" or to "achieve" forget the major principles which need to be applied within a lifetime in order to feel happy and fulfilled. The temporary pressures of feeling good have begun to be blurred by material possessions and by trying to live up to standards set by someone else. The media gives people the impression that self-image is everything, but then go about destroying what self-image is all about by dictating how people should look, behave and present themselves.

The book gives a lot of examples and also clear advice on all the different aspects of happiness and the state of being happy. While many may judge themselves as being "happy" are they really? The book shows how the different elements which affect happiness can be influenced by positive thought. It even goes as far as suggesting exercises to help people to attain a state of happiness and to understand the method used in positive thinking to overcome obstacles.

If you have the slightest doubt that you have experienced true happiness, the book will help you to work through all of the different aspects which make up the puzzle. It covers life skills, interaction with other people, the way that people see themselves and the way that self-image can be improved to provide happiness. Positivity is the key element which is missing when happiness levels are at an all-time low. The unique approach of the book chapters is to use a system of scales to help readers to understand the complexity of their lives with much more clarity.

Reviews:

Be happy! By Jamie
A QUALITY Book Uncovering the Tools That Lie Within to Find Happiness! By Cathy Wilson

Public speaking is the main principal element of fear for most people. Sometimes, finding one's own voice in front of a crowd can cause a great amount of anxiety and stress. In order to overcome the fear of public speaking, there are different strategies and techniques that one can employ to become a more confident communicator. While some are born with an innate sense of how to speak to an audience, others are scared speechless at the mere idea of giving a speech. Feeling nervous before giving a speech is normal and can be control by following the guidelines outlined in this book.

Don't be discouraged, if you bomb out during your first public speaking engagement; allow us to help you focus on your potential to find your place among the great speakers of the world. After reading this book you will be able to keep the butterflies you feel in check, and to bring your communication skills to greater heights.

Reviews:
Very helpful; highly recommended! By Dan Alatorre
LOVE IT! By Kevin